Prevailing
Love

To Missy Lou
Happy 12th birthday.
For quiet hours of
reflection on our Savior.
Praying for your total
healing. Love Nan

Connie

Prevailing
Love Poems of Faith, Family, and Hope

Constance Howard Moore

TATE PUBLISHING & *Enterprises*

Published by Tate Publishing & Enterprises, LLC
127 E. Trade Center Terrace | Mustang, Oklahoma 73064 USA
1.888.361.9473 | www.tatepublishing.com

Tate Publishing is committed to excellence in the publishing industry. The company reflects the philosophy established by the founders, based on Psalm 68:11,
"The Lord gave the word and great was the company of those who published it."

Book design copyright © 2011 by Tate Publishing, LLC. All rights reserved.
Cover design by Sarah Kirchen
Interior design by Chelsea Womble

Published in the United States of America

ISBN: 978-1-61346-275-1
Poetry, Inspirational & Religious
11.08.08

I dedicate this book to the memory of my mother-in-law, Lorene Johnson. She was a talented but not publicly recognized artist. She made drawings that were included in small homemade booklets of poetry that I put together in the past. Three of her drawings are in this book.

Table of Contents

Section Two: In Relationship and Prayer

Section Three: Family Love

Section Four: Feelings and Frailties

Section Five: Reflections

Section One:

Awesome Father God

You are my mainstay, my anchor,
    A net when I fall.
You are my source of consolation
    And encouragement.
When I was broken,
    You wrapped me in love,
        Smoothed, softened, shaped,
            And quilted my fragments
                Together.

You are an always-flowing fountain.
    Your love is my theme;
        Your shelter, my peace.

You are majestic and intricate.
I see You in the immensity of nature.
You are in the scent of sweet-smelling roses,
    In the rustle of wind-blown oak leaves,
        In a drop of dew on a pine tree needle,
            In the flight of a soaring bird,
                In the surprise of a spring tulip.

I see You in landscapes and skylines.
I see You in the faces of people.
I see You in people reaching out with love.
I see You in beauty around me—and creativity.
I see You in the vastness of the heavens,
	In the sun, the moon, and the clouds passing by.

Thank You.

Becoming

I looked, but I did not see.
I read, but I did not comprehend.
I heard, but I did not listen.
I spoke, saying nothing.
I breathed without living.
Then I welcomed the Spirit of God,
And I began to change.
God breathed His life into me,
And I began to live.
I looked, and I began to see.
I read, and began to understand.
I listened and began to perceive.
I pray, and God communicates,
And beauty is seen and heard,
And beauty is read and spoken,
And I am loved,
Because God is gracious.

He Is

My hand is the pen of a ready writer,
My voice a joyful noise of praise.
My heart overflows with a good theme.
I dedicate my verses to the King.
Who is this King of which I sing?
He is the Lord, strong and mighty.
He is the River of life.
He is the Light of the world.
He is love and the Eternal God.
He is our Source and Creator
And the originator of our faith.
He is holy and worthy of praise.
He is my Savior and Lord.
He is my Protector and Benefactor.
He is the comfort in which I rest.
I am called to praise Him;
In and of myself I cannot, but yet I do.
He is my peace, my contentment,
And my exceedingly great reward.
I cannot but respond to His love.

Constance Howard Moore

My name is in the palm of His hand;
My name is in His book of life.
His Words are in my heart
        As much as I can contain.
I am a frail vessel of clay.
I am water poured out,
            Spilling ink on a page.
He is more than awesome.
Glory forever to the one and only King
            Of all kings.

Inspired partly by Psalm 45:1 and Psalm 24:8–10

A Christmas Vision

On a cold Christmas Eve
With snow falling on trees
I saw a vision—a wonderful sight:
God extended love's hands
And presented His plans
In glorious scenes and circles of light.
His love came descending
With life never ending
And healing for humanity's plight.

The Messiah child lay
In a manger of hay.
His star in the east stood over the earth.
Angels sang from above
Proclaiming God's love,
And shepherds hurried to see what they heard.
They found Jesus, the Christ,
The Creator of life,
And celebrated our Savior's birth.

Wise men followed His star
Traveling from afar
With gifts of frankincense, myrrh, and gold.
They were thankful and praised
For the child that would save
As long ago, great prophets foretold.
The Messiah child grew
In grace and wisdom, too.
His purpose was to make people whole.

In a wilderness dawn
He was baptized by John,
Then resisted temptations and lies.
He went about teaching,
Forgiving, and healing
And gathered followers to His side.
He opened people's eyes,
Answered desperate cries,
And depended on His Father as guide.

He took a boy's fish and bread,
Blessed and multiplied them—
And fed thousands on a mountainside.

He faced opposition,
Completed His mission—
Rejected—denied—then crucified.
He arose from the grave
So that we might be saved,
And whoever believed would have life.

Intricacy

God spoke and gave birth to Heaven and Earth.
He said, "Let there be . . ." and it became.
He made light and darkness and day and night.
He adorned the skies with lights and birds of flight.
He's the Father who gathered waters into seas.
He made earth blossom with grass, herbs, and trees.
He put the beauty of the moon in the twilight of the sky.
He spoke just so and made the glow of sunset and sunrise.
He made clouds and lightning and thunderclaps.
He even made the cat that cuddles in my lap
    And squirrels that play in my trees.
He carved canyons and rivers majestically.
He made deer, wolves, goats, and the cattle on a thousand hills.
He made the song of whippoorwills and the beauty of sweet daffodils.
He is the Rock and made the rocks and mountain tops
    From the tiniest to the huge.

He made the sand on every shore and all that's in each sea.
He spoke the plains into being and the golden wheat.
He breathed valleys, butterflies, and the leaves on each tree,
And from the dust of the earth He created a vapor that's uniquely me.

Constance Howard Moore

God Sees

God sees like a gardener.
    He sees all the weeds.
He sees our broken stems
    And each new leaf.
He knows my selfishness
    And He sees my greed.
He sees my self-pride
    And knows my deceit.
He sees in the darkness
    And sees in the light.
He knows what I'm doing
    Whether wrong or right.
He sees like a general
    With spies in the streets.
He sees who I run with
    Wherever we meet.
He sees in the casino;
    He sees where I go;
Whatever I do,
    He already knows.

He watches over the earth
   To see who He can bless.
He calls all the weary
   And offers them rest.
He sees like a father
   With a prodigal son.
He knows all our faults
   But sees us through love.
God sees us through Jesus,
   Our Savior and friend.
He sees us, His children,
   Depending on Him.

The Fire of Life

I haven't always been aware
Of the presence in the fire of life
Of my Lord and Savior, Jesus Christ.
I haven't always known He cared.

I was never far from His sight.
He warned and gently tried to persuade;
Yet always let me go my own way.
When asked, He helped me with my life.

He was near at hand by my side
Even in times when I turned away;
He waited for me to come and pray,
Ready to hear my heartfelt cry.

I was a broken pot of clay,
Sinking, smothered in thickening mire,
Burning in a smelting furnace fire.
He was there to save when I prayed.

He breathed on me His holy fire.
He took my hand and pulled me through.
He mended, remolded, made me new.
Now I'm a child in His Empire.

The Spirit of Jesus

He helps us in our weaknesses
And helps each one to pray.
He searches our hearts and minds
And knows what we need to say.
He works for good in everything
And stays close by our side.
With knowledge of God's own good will
He seeks to be our guide.
He speaks with love and calls to love
And never-ending peace.
Through hardship, pain, and suffering
His love will never cease.
He helps us daily overcome
And lifts us when we're down.
With perseverance, sure and true,
He leads us Heaven-bound.

Inspired by Romans 8:26–28, 35–39

His Story Continues

His story doesn't stop at the Cross;
His life doesn't end with the grave.
The stone, then and now, is rolled away,
And He lives today to help and save.

He died crucified on the Cross,
But He doesn't remain that way.
He rose forgiving from the grave,
And He lives where we live today.

He walked in our steps before the Cross;
He knows our feelings and needs.
He reigns in glory, resides on earth,
And He always intercedes.

His blood is wine flowing from the Cross,
A river of life in eternity.
He works through people like you and me,
And His bread is to help humanity.

Constance Howard Moore

He isn't hanging now on the Cross;
He was there only a few hours,
But the work of the Cross is forever
Bringing hope and peace in His power.

His story only paused at the Cross,
A time when He suffered and bled
So we could drink of His life-giving wine
And eat of His healing bread.

Heavenly Care

The Lord is near to those who call;
He lifts them when they fall.
He is always present to help;
He calls to us himself.

He longs for us and knows our names;
He loves each one the same.
The Lord forgives whoever asks;
His mercies last and last.

Forever His kindness endures;
His love is faithful and sure.
He leads and heals and knows what's best;
His way is peace and rest.

Constance Howard Moore

Green Melodies

Lavender blush on redbud trees
Humming tunes of fresh, tender buds
And lush, light green leaves—
A soft music picture of serenity.

Dogwood blooms cling to bare limbs,
Piccolo puffs of floating white clouds;
A white lace chorus serenades the birth of spring
And harmonizes with advancing green.

Mimosa blooms reach skyward,
Soft pink on feathery green;
Floating blooms dance with the wind,
Singing secret summer songs.

Shimmering sunlight flutters through tall trees,
A living paisley on xylophone leaves.
Green and gold waltz together,
Descending and ascending between earth and sky.

I know there's music;
I see the rhythm and feel the beat.
It's the same and changes day to day,
And it's always new.

I wonder. Is music everywhere?
Songs of life and beauty and praise.
Are angels on earth singing glory to God?
It must be too wonderful for human ears.

Inspired by 1 Chronicles 16:33a

Because God Loves

Because God loves,
He makes His love gifts available.
His love is the oxygen in fresh air
And a buffet feast with sparkling water
    And a bottle of wine.

God's love is a flower garden,
A vegetable garden,
Rivers of flowing living water,
Help climbing mountains,
And comfort and rest in valleys.

God's love is glue to the earth,
The atmosphere, and all that we are.
His Word created the earth and everything,
And holds everything He created together.

God's love is healing salve for broken hearts
And broken lives; it's splints for broken bones.
It's a hospital for repair, rebuilding, and recuperation.

It's shelter in a jungle, an oasis in a desert,
Bread from Heaven in a wilderness,
And a land of Goshen till we're called out of Egypt.

God's love is the Light of the world,
A bright candle shining in darkness,
And rooms glowing with love.
Accepting God's love is a heaven connection.
God's love is Jesus.

Autumn Beauty

A soft concert of gentle sounds
    A waltz of leaves and wind
Trees releasing valued treasure
    Gold leaf rain drifting down
Sunshine magic and illusion
    Sunset of the seasons
Strands of gold lie in the road
    Richer than rainbow's end
Abundant color everywhere
    A tapestry of time and wealth
A time of beauty—a time of peace
    A time of slowing down
A time of quiet renewal
    A time of growth at rest
A time to appreciate
    God's creation of autumn
    And His glory in its beauty

His Way

He needed to come to Samaria,
A place along His way;
He spoke to a woman with a past,
An outcast of her day.
He asked for water and offered water—
Life-giving living water.
He was the Christ; His bread was doing
The will of His Father.

He came and comes to me in my need;
He helps me when I pray.
Whatever the situation might be,
He is the only way.
He gives me love and cups of water—
Life-giving living water.
May I follow in His steps and do
The will of my Father.

He comes to various places
Seeming out of His way;

Constance Howard Moore

He offers acceptance and speaks to all,
Any time, night or day.
He is a friend and comes with water—
Life-giving living water.
He is the Christ, the risen Messiah,
The Son of the Father.

Inspired by John 4:4–42

The Greatest Love

Oh, for the love of God,
    The love of Christ,
To fill and overflow
That we might recognize
And more fully know
The love of God, gracious and giving,
    Unconditional, compassionate,
        Helpful, and kind,
            Gently nudging, never forcing,
Always welcoming,
Turning no one away,
    Undeserved, full of mercy,
    Forgiving and good,
Unearned,
    The Father's endowment,
    The legacy of the Son,
    The love gift of life,
    And above and beyond,
    And exceedingly additional,
    And even more,

My efforts all failed, but, oh, it was fun
    In fellowship with the glorious Almighty One,
        And awesome to think of all He has done.
I thought of a grandfather with a child on his knee,
    And my loving daddy playing games with me,
And a loved little toddler toddling after his dad,
        And children at play, all laughing and glad,
        And very good gifts and ships underway,
        And peace and contentment all of my days.

But God Waited

Beautiful, young, godly women,
I envy your energy and bubbliness,
The effervescence of God flowing in you.
I feel tired and flat and worn out.
I married too young and had babies too soon.
I married a wrong man;
I was ignorant and stupid, naïve and gullible.
I was drawn by blind chemical lust
And thought it was love.
I wasn't in tune with God;
I wasn't listening to or leaning on Him.
He let me turn and go my own way,
And I have suffered for it and suffer some still.

But God waited on high for my return;
He waited that He might be gracious to me.
He waited for me to seek and exalt Him.
He waited for me to return and rest in Him.
He waited to hold, help, and strengthen me.
He waited to fill me with quietness and confidence.

He has blessed me magnificently.
He has been and is gracious to me,
And I believe will forever be gracious to me
And all those who turn and return to Him.
Is He waiting to be gracious to you?

Partly inspired by a Christian ladies meeting with several young Christian women, some of my life experience, and Isaiah 30:15, 18–19

God Is Everything to Me

The air I breathe,
    The song in my heart,
        Peace of mind.
Rest in the night,
    A light in the dark,
        The break of dawn.
A refreshing spring breeze,
    Smiles and laughter,
        Illumination.
Hope and happiness,
    Love and forgiveness,
        And release from guilt.
A place of shelter,
    A new beginning,
        Healing and restoration.
Consolation,
    Encouragement,
        Sunset and sunrise.

Infinity,
    Today and tomorrow,
      Forever.
God is everything to me.
It is to Him I sing.

Solace

Soothing salve to my soul,
Healing for my hurting heart,
Comfort when things go wrong,
Consolation in disappointments.

He is my God, my King, my everything;
He is my consolation.
He provides for me magnificently;
No other could suffice.

His Word is true and good.
His Word is love and life.
His Word heals and builds and rebuilds.
His Word is everlasting.

He is faithful to His Word.
He is faithful to His promises.
He is my refuge and mainstay.
He is my source and comfort.

Inspired by Psalm 94:19 and Psalm 147:3

A Love Song of Praise

I love You, Lord God;
You are bread and wine
And substance in my life.
You are laughter and gold
And friendship to my soul.
You are pleasant, flowing streams,
Encouragement and dreams.
You are patience and peace
And a daily faithful feast.
You are gentle and strong;
You are help when things go wrong.
You are salt and candlelight
Adding meaning to my life.
You are music and ballet
Growing sweeter every day.
You are dewdrops on green leaves,
And a soothing summer breeze.
You are shelter in the cold
And warmth within my soul.
You are sunshine in my mind,

Always caring, always kind.
You are rest and liberation;
You are my inspiration.
I love You, Lord God.

Magnificent Mercy

God's mercy is magnificent and great.
When we turn to Him, He forgives our evil ways.
He sets us on high and gives us a place
Among all the other eternal saints.

Woe to those who turn from righteousness.
Woe to those who turn to evil ways.
Woe to those who turn from the Lord.
Their righteousness will be forgotten and their evil
repaid.
May they return to the Lord before it's too late.

The day of the Lord is coming sometime soon.
Who will be prepared? Who will be afraid?
Are you washed in His blood and doing His Word?
Do you walk in His mercy and dwell in His grace?
Do you have a place among eternal saints?

God takes no pleasure in anyone's death.
His mercy warns and calls to repentance.

His mercy forgives, lifts, and gives grace.
God's mercy teaches the way of the saints.
God's mercy is magnificent and great.

Inspired by Ezekiel 18:21–32 and Ephesians 2:1–13

Constance Howard Moore

Passion

He is the Lamb for me and you,
A perfect lamb, sacrificed.
A crown of thorns crushed His head,
And His back was cruelly beaten.
Nails pierced His hands and feet.
He suffered and bled for me and you.

He paid the price,
    And set things right,
        And paved the way to a better life.
He covered our sin with sacrifice,
    Wrapped us in love,
        And drew us to Him.
If we respond,
    I hope with a yes,
        We have heavenly hope in Him.

He is the answer; He is the guide;
He is the one who knows what's right.
He provides life on Earth and also in Heaven.

His is the glory and His is the praise.
He's the Creator, who gives us each day.
He's the Good Shepherd, and He is the Way.

Constance Howard Moore

He Sent His Word

Because God loves, He sent His Word.
He sent His Word to instruct and encourage
 And help us know Him.
He sent His Word to help us learn.
He sent His Word to be near at hand,
 In our mouths and in our hearts.
He sent His Word to light our path
 And show us the way
 And guide us each from day to day.
He sent His Word to answer our cry
 And respond to our needs.
He sent His Word to deliver.
He sent His Word to save and heal,
 To give us faith and help us believe.
He sent His Word and Jesus, His Son,
 To bring light into darkness
 And life to everyone.

Inspired by Deuteronomy 30:14 and Psalm 107:19–20

God Gives

God gives the gift of the Holy Spirit
Like gentle, soothing rain after a drought
Thoughtfully filling emptiness
With living water flowing from His Word.

God gives Christ on the Cross
And Christ resurrected.
He gives deep wells of salvation
With living water flowing from His Word.

God gives light in darkness and in confusion.
He gives compassion and loving kindness.
He gives meditations of love and healing
With living water flowing from His Word.

God gives His Word and all we need.
He gives and gives and gives, graciously.
He gives to all who are willing to receive
Living water flowing freely from His Word.

Constance Howard Moore

A Choice

Let's give God the credit;
Let's give Him His due.
He's the Creator
And He made me and you.
He made all the Earth
And the Heavens, too.
He holds them together
With His special glue.

God created our bodies
And gave us our minds.
He gave us His Word
And His will for our lives.
He gives us a choice:
To live or to die,
To follow His guidance
Or all that is lies.

God created the darkness.
He created the light.
He created each day

And also each night.
He knows what we need
And knows what is right.
He gives us a choice
And urges: choose life.

God gives good guidance
To all who will hear.
He knows our whole heart
And He's always near.
He's the source of our lives
And His love is clear.
We are His children
And to Him we are dear.

God is our Father.
He's the Most High.
He's the Almighty,
And He never lies.
We can go our own way
Or walk by His side.
He gives us a choice:
To live or to die.

Inspired by Deuteronomy 30:19 and Micah 6:8

Constance Howard Moore

Praising God

You are so good.
You are so kind.
You are so loving.
You are peace in my mind.

You are amazing.
You are great.
You are mercy,
And You are grace.

I'll praise You forever,
Though my words aren't enough.
I find joy in Your presence
And delight in Your love.

You are songs in my heart
And joy in my day.
You are hope everlasting
And peace leading the way.

You are Father to me
And none can compare.
You are comfort and life
And beauty to share.

I'm in awe of You.
Your Word is supreme.
You dazzle my heart.
You are Father and King.

Section Two:

In Relationship and Prayer

My Life's Fabric

The fabric of my life
Is a rough knobby tweed
Of irregular weave
Interwoven by Christ.

If my fabric should tear,
Christ is most enduring;
He's always assuring;
He's present to repair.

He's willing to reweave
A broken, bleeding heart,
My fabric torn apart,
Or a hole in my sleeve.

In Life's Difficulties

In times of stress
And times of duress
I bow at Father God's feet.

I cling to the Cross
When all seems lost
And my efforts are in vain.

He provides peace
And gently leads
And kindly comforts my heart.

I call on His name;
He's my only claim
To anything in this life.

He gives me grace
And helps me face
Whatever may come my way.

Constance Howard Moore

He holds my hand
And helps me stand
And do what needs to be done.

All I Can Do

All I can do is go back to the Cross;
Place there my suffering, my pain, and my loss,
My weakness, my longing, my penitent heart,
Then accept each day as a fresh, new start.

Thinking on Jesus and all that He did,
I remember He's faithful to forgive.
In Him I have hope; in Him I have peace.
His love is far greater than I can perceive.

I need His love; I need His comfort;
I need His Word as water in my desert.
I need Him first, foremost, and always.
He's the crux of my life; I am His clay.

All I can do is start over once more;
Try to do better than I did before.
All I can do is begin again,
Resting in Jesus as helper and friend.

Constance Howard Moore

Inspired by 1 Peter 5:6–7. I had fallen into the trap of self-pride and was humbled by a huge disappointment.

Big

Big boulder worries, big boulder concerns,
Burdens I can't bear alone.
I look to the Light, to Jesus Christ,
And humble myself before Him.
I share my cares and share my concerns;
I share my worries and woes;
I share my troubles and even my tears;
I lay all before Him like a dearest best friend.
He lifts and carries my burdens and me.
My worries seem slight in His mighty hands.
It's a miraculous wonder and I don't understand,
But all seems small when placed in His hands,
And life is so very much lighter.

Inspired by 1 Peter 5:6–7

The Time

Enjoy each moment from day to day
For now is the time that we live;
Now is the time to work and play,
The time to be kind and forgive.
We cannot redo what's done and gone;
"If onlys" are only a dream.
Today is the time to sing a song
And dance in each sunbeam.
One step at a time, line upon line,
We live each day but one day.
May we make the most of all our time
And the most of what comes our way.
Now is the time to have faith and stand
And the time to do our best,
To do whatever is in our hands
And trust in God—He'll do the rest.

My husband took a better-paying job that he thought he wanted, but it was wrong for him. He struggled with this job till he was able to go to a lower-paying job simi-

lar to his old job that was more right for him. In this case more money wasn't best. God gave me this poem while my husband was struggling with the better-paying job.

Jesus Calls

Jesus is the Lord Our Righteousness
Jesus is the Vine
Jesus is the Shepherd
He will lead us with His love
Jesus is the Word of God
And the Way of life
Jesus is the Messiah
He calls us all by name

He's the Savior of my heart
And the Lover of my soul
He's the Lifter of my head
And my source of help
He's my peace and my joy
He is grace and graciousness
And forever flowing streams of love
He calls us all to a better life

We're called to believe in Him
We're called to be a praise

We're called to love Him first and always
We're called to live by faith
We're called to delight in Him
And meditate on His Word
We're called to seek His counsel
And humbly walk with Him

After I wrote this I wondered about it because it seems a little wild. To give me peace about this poem I read the following list of scriptures: Isaiah 43:2, John 16:33, 2 Corinthians 5:17, Psalm 23:3, John 10:7–9, John 14:6, Isaiah 9:6, John 1:1–5, Deuteronomy 31:6, and Hebrews 13:5–6.

Softly

As rain and snow water the earth,
So God's Word is water to me;
It's encouragement and healing;
It's a word of advice and wisdom book
With examples and treachery and all that is human;
It points to Jesus, the Light, and all that's right.

As sunshine warms and nurtures the earth,
So God's Son is sunshine to me.
He's salvation and comfort and eternal peace.
He's my advocate and Heavenly home.
He's warmth in the cold and cooling in heat.
He's the Teacher as I sit at His feet.

As the wind whispers softly in the trees,
So my Savior speaks softly to me,
Words of wisdom and endless love.
He satisfies with songs in the night,
Songs of deliverance and songs of delight,
Songs of assurance and verses to write.

Constance Howard Moore

My Daffodils

These are my daffodils, bobbing in the sun,
This is my beauty, my pleasure, my fun:
Thanking God for creation; thanking Him for His love;
Giving praise to the Father and praise to the Son.

These are my daffodils, yellow and white,
Refreshing and pretty, a springtime delight:
Delight in my Savior and His shining light;
Delight in the morning and through each dark night.

These are my daffodils, all dancing with glee,
Silent trumpets in a sweet melody;
These are my daffodils: my Father and me
Communing in union with harmony.

These are my daffodils: the music of praise
With the methodical rhythm of day to day,
In both the marvelous and the mundane.
My daffodils all sing in sunshine and rain.

Going Beyond

He was a carpenter's son, who went beyond
What appeared to be His destiny
To eyes of people like you and me.

He was and is God's one and only Son,
Who can in His power bring us beyond
What appears to be our destiny.

He was and is the risen Messiah,
The One who vanquished Satan's spell,
The One who conquered death and hell.

All honor, glory, and power are His.
Let's humbly bow and learn from Him
And receive His Spirit and be in Him.

Let's walk in His shadow where we belong.
Let's fellowship at His side and in Him;
Let's dwell in His Word and glory in Him.

Constance Howard Moore

Let's seek His face and submit to Him.
Let's receive His peace and rest in Him
And go beyond what seems to be our destiny.

Inspired by Jeremiah 32:17

In Christ

In Christ I am special,
    But not on my own.
With Him all is possible;
    I'm useless alone.
To Him be the glory;
    To Him be the praise.
I must give Him credit
    For good every day.
In Christ I am loved,
    Forgiven, and clean.
In Christ I'm made whole;
    In Him I'm complete.

Constance Howard Moore

Building Stones

Straight backs, strong bones,
Lively living building stones,
All ringing, singing a tune
Honoring the Builder
And Chief Corner Stone.

Bonded forever,
Fitly joined together,
Yielding to others.
Unique, yet the same.
Weak alone, strong together.

Temple treasure,
Part of the Builder's pleasure.
In relationship,
Joined with the Corner Stone,
Yielded to the Builder.

Royal, holy, dwelling in light.
Guarded, guided by what's right.

Chosen, valued,
Mended, molded.
Fit as eagles in flight.

Lively living building stones
Patiently placed, not alone.
A temple being built,
Blessed, loved, becoming
Straight backs, strong bones.

Inspired by 1 Peter 2:4–6

Exhortation

Stay out of the darkness;
　　Walk in the light.
Stay close to Jesus;
　　He'll light every night.
Seek after His kingdom;
　　Seek after His face.
Follow His footsteps;
　　Live in His grace.
His way brings blessing;
　　His way brings peace.
His way is ultimate;
　　His way is sweet.
Savor His beauty;
　　Rest in His rest.
Take hold of His hand;
　　His way is best.

Matthew 6:33

An Upper Room

I have an upper room down below,
A place of worship and play.
I praise the Lord and study His Word
And give thanks to Him every day.
He's the Lord of my life and He is King.
I love Him more with each passing day.
He's my hero and He amazes me.
I love His strong, tender, loving ways.
I can do crafts or write or sew
And sing to the Lord in loving praise.
I can exalt Him and lift Him on high
And humble myself and quietly pray.
The garden is also an upper room,
A place of worship and play.
I can trim a bush or pick a flower
Or dig in the dirt and praise.
A peaceful walk is an upper room,
A place of worship and praise,
Of contemplating the glories of nature
And giving God glory and praise.

Constance Howard Moore

Contentment

My heart is seared with peace;
Contentment is my lot.
Though I have many things,
It would be the same if I had naught.
Things can never hold me;
My heart is held by God.

He knows me through and through,
From secret thought to open deed.
He sees both good and bad
And knows my every need.
He calms and comforts me
And keeps me in His peace.

Inspired by Hebrews 13:5

Awake at Night

I have a routine of solitude
In wakeful times at night.
Do not speak; do not intrude.
Do not turn on another light.

I have a reverie of peacefulness,
Of reading and of prayer,
Of quietness to sleepiness
In the peacefulness of God's care.

Constance Howard Moore

My Guide Book—
The Bible

I have a great little guide book,
    Several books in one.
It helps me know which way to go
    When following the Son.
It helps me with the curves in life;
    It helps me overcome.
It helps me try to do my best
    And helps me do what's right.
It shows me how I'm truly loved,
    And how to sing at night.
It tells me where to run and rest,
    And leads me to the Light.
It leads me in a peaceful way
    And helps me having fun.
My guide book is a joy to read
    And share with anyone.
With my guide book I'm improving,
    But I've only just begun.

Bible Study

A Bible study is a muscleman workout
And muscle-building food for spirit and soul
To help Christians grow stronger.
It's a green plateau growing lilies of the field
And a child in the lap of a loving father.
It's humbly sitting at our Savior's feet
And learning and growing in the Way of life.
It's a prodigal son who turns out to be good.
It's examples of people as human as me
And examples of people with God shining through.
Bible study is revelations of love,
Daily bread and provision in drought,
Encouragement, comfort, and hope.
It's a road map, road signs, and a bright flashlight.
It's the fear of the Lord
And guidance for life.
It's the beginning of knowledge
And the beginning of wisdom.
A Bible study is trees clapping their hands,

Flowers looking to the sun and praising God,
And people growing in the soil of God's love.
It's prayer and praise to the Most High
And a worthy endeavor that's God approved.

A Good Pastor

He's not a man of leisure
    Who sits around to boast.
He's a hard-working, busy man
    Without time to loaf.
He laughs, smiles, and has a good time;
    He enjoys his everyday life.
He counts it joy when trials come
    And truly is in Christ.
He believes in doing what's right,
    Every time in every place.
He teaches and preaches, sharp and clear;
    The Bible is his base.
He studies, mulls, and quotes God's Word;
    He's flexible in God's hands.
He truly cares about his flock,
    And helps whenever he can.
He doesn't conform to the ways of this world;
    He isn't filled with pride.
He's humbly centered in God's Word
    And humbly centered in Christ.

Guard and Help Me

Lord, guard me, please, from myself,
From self-pride and self-sufficiency,
And the sad mess I'd be on my own.

Guard me from deception
And the evilness of greed
And the needless shame of guilt.

I shudder to think of what might have been,
And where I might still be if not for Christ,
And all the disaster that could have been.

Help me dress myself in humility,
And clothe myself in Christ,
And be humble before You all my life.

Thank You, Lord, for value in You,
And who I am in Christ,
And love and life and everything good.

Abundant Life

Is life entwined with the Overcomer
Hope more faithful than spring and summer
Staying afloat on each stormy sea

The Word of God alive in my heart
Knowing His love will never depart
Forgiveness for all the wrong I've done

God's goodness overlaying what's bad
Happiness when everything seems sad
Peace and comfort in times of distress

Not worrying what tomorrow brings
Fellowship with the King of all kings
Yielding daily to a better way

Commonplace purpose for being alive
Having an ever-present, all-knowing guide
Praising the Lord with songs in my heart

Forever Happiness

Rejoicing in the work of the Cross
　　And the birth of Christ.
Rejoicing in the willingness of Mary
　　And the obedience of Joseph.
Rejoicing with the joy and wonder
　　Of the shepherds that night.
Singing and being lifted with angels
　　In sanctuaries of praise.
Emulating the wise ones
　　Following His star.
Drawing near, being thankful, worshipping,
　　In spirit and in truth.
Giving and receiving, remembering
　　The birth, the Christ, the Cross,
The Alpha and the Omega.

Inspired by Philippians 4:4

God's Love Is Forever

Through difficulties, hardship, and grief,
    His love remains steadfast.
If we profit and do well,
    His love is also there.
If we forget and turn to ourselves
    Or other things or other ways,
He waits on High for our return.
    His love doesn't go away.
He wants to be gracious and show mercy.
    He wants our trust to be in Him.
He's a God of justice with guidance to give,
    And He truly knows what's best.

Inspired by Romans 8:35–39 and Isaiah 30:15, 18

Constance Howard Moore

The Bread of Life

As we read God's Word with all our heart and an open mind,
And season our reading with prayer,
It becomes the living water of life and deep wells of salvation.
As we continue our reading in God's Word,
Water becomes wine and fullness of joy,
And wells of wine become rivers of life.
God's Word becomes our Bread of life,
And we are nourished by the Bread of life.
We comingle with the Word become flesh,
Who dwells among us.
We become branches of love, reflectors of light,
And do the work of believing.
As we read and chew and drink more deeply from God's Word,
It becomes a wedding feast,
Moments of rapture and glimpses of Heaven.
It is miraculous, wonderful, profound,
Amazing, unexplainable, and more.

It is love overflowing, joy in all situations,

And marvelous peace that the world doesn't know.

The Bread of life is sweet, sustaining manna from Heaven.

All are welcome to partake.

Lead Us

Lead us, Lord, in the good times;
    Lead us through the bad.
Lead us when we're happy
    And also when we're sad.

Lead us, Lord, when we're wayward,
    Back into Your fold.
Lead us in Your righteous ways,
    Lead us young and old.

Cleanse our minds from worry;
    Heal us when we're sick.
Lead us in our daily walk
    On paths that benefit.

Teach us, Lord, words of peace;
    Help us do what's right.
Lead us, Lord, every day;
    Keep us in Your sight.

Be our shield and shelter;
  Light our darkest hours.
Lead us to a pleasant place
  Filled with fruit and flowers.

Feed us, Lord, with Your manna;
  Warm us when we're cold.
Lead us through each valley
  To greener lands of gold.

Lead us, lead us, lead us, Lord,
  In the way that we should go.
Lead us, Lord; we love You;
  Help us learn and grow.

Constance Howard Moore

In the Sunshine
and the Rain

God's grace helps me each morning,
Helps me with my daily life.
Trees grow tall and flowers bloom
In the sunshine and the rain.

Children grow; they laugh; they cry.
Hardship adds its part to life.
Days go by and life goes on
In the sunshine and the rain.

God's grace lends tranquility.
Happiness flowers within.
May we love and live life well
In the sunshine and the rain.

Each moment is a jewel;
Some are diamonds in the rough.
Treasure is in all of life
In the sunshine and the rain.

Earth remains magnificent;
Her beauty shines everywhere,
If we see or if we don't,
In the sunshine and the rain.

God provides and makes a way.
Trees grow tall and flowers bloom;
May we too do just as well
In the sunshine and the rain.

Section Three:

Family Love

It Was Mercy

I didn't know; I couldn't see;
I was blinded by adversity.
Strife and sickness struggled and schemed
As a strong, stormy, united team.
Mercy took my dear son away
To a safe, more pleasant, loving place.
On raging seas my house was tossed
With windows open and doors unlocked.
I had as much as I could bear
Without a troubled teenager's care.

I didn't know; I couldn't see;
I was blinded by adversity.
A storm-tossed house breaking apart;
My son and daughter tore at my heart.
Mercy took my dear son away,
Then held me together night and day.
Mercy raised my sails to the wind
While beckoning storm clouds to rescind.
Mercy healed my daughter and me,
Provided peace on a raging sea.

Inspired by Psalm 103:11, 17. Our diabetic daughter came home for rest and recuperation after passing out in the library at college. Her presence and health problems added stress to our already troubled household. We sent our son to live with my sister in Florida, where he graduated from high school.

Constance Howard Moore

Remember Me

Gracious God, who gives all good gifts,
God of love, blessing, and benefits,
Almighty God, reigning on High,
Lord of the universe, hear my cry.
As You honor Your Word, promises true,
Remember me, I'm depending on You.
Remember my husband, who's faithful to me;
Reveal Yourself magnificently.
Cause us to flourish, staying fresh and new,
Always learning and growing with You.
Remember my children. You love them too;
They also have dreams coming from You.
Bless our efforts, fulfill our desires,
Touch our lives, lifting us higher.
I have faith in Your Word, and I believe.
Grant my request and help us receive.

Empathy for
My Daughter

Bound in a body that doesn't fit,
My spirit soars while my body sits.
All the world is open to me,
Though my body is bound by infirmity.
I've a mind alert and bright,
And my eyes are opened by the light.
My spirit rejoices and I happily sing,
Yet my body doesn't do many things.
My spirit leaps and jumps for joy,
While my body remains infirmity's toy.
My mind is filled with fabulous dreams,
Thoughts and ideas flow in perpetual streams.
Oh, body of mine, come in line with me,
Be released from shackles of infirmity.

When I wrote this, our diabetic daughter was recovering
from having part of her foot amputated. She spent most

of her time in an easy chair with her feet on an ottoman. Home health came regularly to check and bandage her foot. It took a long time for her foot to heal.

A Caring Brother

I looked, I saw, and I was pleased
    On that September day.
You took your sister's arm in yours
    And helped her on her way.
Caring love was in your manner,
    Tenderness in your touch.
You took your sister's arm in yours
    And helped her with her steps.
My heart was touched, a mother's heart;
    I almost shed a tear.
You shared yourself and your dreams.
    My heart remembers well;
I watched with awe and joyful heart
    On that September day.
You took your sister's arm in yours
    And helped her on her way.

What a joy for a mother to see her children interact with love. We took our adult disabled daughter, who was partially blind, to see the new house that our oldest son and his wife were building; it was almost completed. Outside the house the ground was rough. Our son took his sister by the hand and showed her around outside and inside the house. I watched them interact from a distance and was so moved by my son's tenderness toward his sister that I almost cried.

Mother Was Gone

He mowed Mother's lawn
I tended Mother's flowers
I unlocked Mother's door
We entered Mother's house
Mother was gone

He didn't notice—he wasn't aware
I crossed intangible emotional barriers
Intruding in Mother's ambiance
Walking in a fog of memory and feelings
Mother's steps matched mine
Mother called from the walls

Mother glanced from a mirror
Mother's eyes pierced mine
Mother's reflection was clear
Mother's voice echoed strong
Mother resounded from ceiling to floor
Mother called from the walls

Constance Howard Moore

Mother lay on her bed
Mother sat in her chairs
Mother read from her books
Mother spoke from her pictures
Mother touched and embraced
Mother called from the walls

Memories were overwhelming
Mother was in her dishes and glasses and pans
Mother was at her sink and at her stove
Mother's teapot whistled—Mother's cat meowed
Mother talked with a child
Mother called from the walls

I drank a glass of water
Mother's house was fine
We left Mother's house
I locked Mother's door
Mother was gone

Mother was a matriarch, a dominant personality and influence in my life. She was my mother, who gave birth to me, raised me, prayed for me, took me to church, read to me, sent me to school, taught me to sew, and took care of me when I was sick. I was told she taught me nursery rhymes when I was three; I don't remember. To me Mother's strong personality permeated all that she had and everything she had spoke of her. Mother's house proclaimed Mother. I've often wondered why her presence didn't permeate her yard and flowers; I think flowers might be so full of God's presence and traces of His glory that there isn't room for anyone else's presence to permeate them.

When I wrote this poem she was in another town with my dad, who was working there. He was a pipeline welder, which involved a lot of travel, work in different places, and periods of unemployment. They always maintained a home in Oklahoma. My husband and I took care of their yard and flowers when they were gone. I always considered their home Mother's house; she spent more time there, and there was more of her in the house. I resemble my mother, so it was easy to see her in my reflection in her mirror. Her pictures were oil paintings that she painted. She loved her cats and even cooked for them. She adored her grandchildren. It was like she was actually there, only she wasn't. She was out of town all summer.

A Jewel

A jewel became tarnished;
A jewel became dim;
A jewel was damaged
Again and again.

A jewel was recalled
From affliction and pain
To be pampered and polished,
Renewed and maintained.

A jewel shines in the Master's house;
A jewel shines bright in the night sky;
A jewel shines in another setting,
A setting apart, away from my life.

I've reminders and thoughts
And moments of why;
Why was she broken?
And why did she die?

Mistakes and mistakes
And faulty earthly clay;
Morning and evening
And a fatal day.

I've glimmers and shadows
And reflections of love;
I've memories and pictures
And gifts that are hugs.

She was bitter and sweet
And love without reason;
She's a tear on my cheek,
My child for a season.

Our daughter became diabetic at age nine. As an adult she had increasing health problems. She was thirty-seven when she died. The last months of her life were spent in the hospital, and most of that was in intensive care.

Remembering

Somebody died and Heaven cried;
    Tears mingled with rain.
Somebody cried, hurt deep inside,
    Could hardly bear the pain.

Gorgeous flowers and lonely hours;
    Trees point to the sky.
Fading showers and wilting flowers;
    It hurts to say good-bye.

I remember the day Laura died,
A Saturday when Heaven cried.

Her house plants died and no one cried;
    Nobody suffered pain.
Her ivy's alive, planted outside,
    Memories with the rain.

Days go by and I often cry.
    The day she died it rained.

I look to the sky, hurting inside.
  God is soothing my pain.

It rained in July when Laura died,
A soft, misty rain while Heaven cried.

My daughter died and Heaven cried;
  Tears mingle with rain.
Her mother cries, more healed inside,
  Able to bear the pain.

Garden flowers nurtured by showers,
  Therapy day by day.
God's holy power heals by the hour,
  Wiping my tears away.

I remember the day Laura died.
It was for me that Heaven cried.

*Laura died July 11, 1998. I wrote this two or three years
after her death, probably after what I call a grief attack.
I was thinking of her and my grief and recovery after her
death.*

Constance Howard Moore

I Love You

When someone close dies,
    The world changes.
Love becomes more precious.
"I love you" takes on new meaning.
Saying "I love you" is more important,
    More urgent, necessary, and vital.
I must say "I love you" to those I love.
I might not see or talk with them again.
We plan, we hope, we dream and pray,
But we don't know what tomorrow brings.
My life without love would be meaningless.
Love is vital to my well-being.
Love expressed
    And time shared are important.
Love is heart food, soul food, health food,
A magnificent, awesome gift.
Love is a God blessing.
I love you.

First Thoughts on Love

Love is a loose knot.
Love allows, relates, communicates,
Doesn't berate or manipulate.
Love considers, never binds,
Love is gentle, love is kind;
Love enhances peace of mind.
Love is willing to be there;
Love listens and wants to share.
Love has no rigid lines.
Love is a loose knot.

Continued Thoughts on Love

Love can't be bought; love can't be sold;
Love is worth more than precious gold.
Love is encouragement and prayer.
Love is constant and always cares.

Love is faithful and secure.
Love believes and endures.
Love considers and communicates.
Love is hope and faith and a warm embrace.

Love shelters but doesn't confine.
Love is gentle; love is kind.
Love enhances peace of mind;
Love is a branch in the Vine.

Love is in sunshine, rain, and a pretty flower,
And a life submitted under God's power.
Love is God ordained and defined by God,
For God is love and love is God.

Inspired by 1 Corinthians 13:4–8a, Matthew 22:37–40, John 13:34–35, John 15:5, 9–12. This poem is a years later version of "First Thoughts on Love," which I still like. I was thinking more of the marriage relationship when I wrote the first version and more on brotherly love or God love when I wrote this second version. I think the last version is the best.

Sentimental Old Men
—My Dad

What is in the packet that old men carry?
Have you seen it? Have you noticed?
Living pictures—and gray pictures
Circling on shelves in their minds—
A grin, a smile, a mischievous look,
A twinkle in his eye—or a tear,
Wild times with other boys,
Home, hunger, and fields of grain,
Cars, road maps, and driving,
Flowers for his sweetheart wife,
Cooing babies and first steps,
Carnivals, circuses, and county fairs,
Replayed words of small children,
Football games, car races, and fishing,
Afternoon and morning naps,
Games with great-grandchildren,
Sickness, health, hospitals, and death,
Failures, successes, and stories not told,
Wise words and foolishness,
War time wounds and medals.

Visits of Value

Visits of value are visits that lift.
I see them as good, sent by God as a gift.
Though trapped in a mind of shortened dimension
She liked visits of love and visits of fun.
She might not remember your name,
But welcomed you grandly just the same.
You were welcomed for sure without a doubt,
And it didn't much matter what you talked about.
She'd remember a visit but not what you said
As she sat in a wheelchair or lay on her bed.

She sadly resided in a nursing home room,
But someone came in and sang her a tune.
They lifted her spirit and made her heart glad,
And made her forget all that was sad.
She was lifted by a stranger's tune
And forgot, for a time, her nursing home room.
Her special feelings lasted for days.
I think God was touching her in loving ways
Through visits of value and visits that lift
And visits of love, sent by Him as a gift.

Constance Howard Moore

This was one of my grandmothers. The stranger that sang her a tune was a singer on a country western television show. She felt like someone came personally into her room and sang to her. I thought that was great and sort of like making the best of a poor situation.

A Child That Was

Once my child,
No longer mine,
A passing segment
Of another time.

A mended whole,
An empty chair,
A candle not lit;
He doesn't care.

He left as a child.
He's gone as a man,
Not made, not broken—
Pride is his stand.

Self is his world,
His life, his pain.
Pride is his prison;
He's shackled and chained.

Constance Howard Moore

Remembered,
No longer missed,
The child I enjoyed,
The baby I kissed.

Joy became mourning
And mourning is gone.
He goes his own way
And sings his own song.

I believe—
In time he'll turn,
Surrender his pride,
Die some to self,
And gain new life.

I believe—
In time he'll live
With humility;
Broken and remolded;
God's child set free.

I believe—
In time he'll learn
To take credit and blame,
Own his mistakes,
And make positive change.

Inspired by 2 Timothy 1:12. Our youngest son is an alcoholic; he separated himself from his family. I wrote this in 2007.

Lovers in Love
and Marriage

A hands-on experience of yielding to each other
With no one intent on dominating the other.
Separate unique individuals woven together
In a harmony of intertwining taste and touch
With single notes individually sung,
And the rising aroma of sweet, pleasing love.
Melodies of give and take, glue to chords of love,
Blended, becoming a symphony of experience,
A medley of the bonding music of lovers in love.
Discord overcome by caring consideration.
Adversity transcended by resourceful unity.
Division banished by warm togetherness.
All forming an orchestration of mutuality,
Mingled with the restful lulls of a peaceful waltz,
Flavored by intermittent rhythms of ecstasy.

Thank God for Love

Thank God for the gift of love,
    For our love for each other.
Thank God for togetherness
    And empty hours filled with joy.
Thank God for the pleasure of your company
    And dreams and hopes and plans.
Thank God for the present,
    Our past, and our future.
Thank God for hardship strengthening our love
    And drawing us closer.
Thank God for good times, humor, and levity
    Enhancing and adding balance.
Thank God for the beauty we see
    In each other, in life, and creation.
Thank God for love.

Constance Howard Moore

The Angel Box

An engraved tin treasure box with a hinged lid
Containing treasures from times past,
Each wrapped protectively in a piece of torn sheet:
An American flag from his Vietnam truck,
And a helmet cover,
A photograph of father and toddler son
Reclining together on a sofa,
And oldest of all—
The angel from ancient early childhood past,
Richly endowed with sentiment—not my own.
Each year she adorns our Christmas tree;
He refuses to have her replaced.
Her beauty lies mostly within.
She's worn out, redressed and redone
Many times over by various loved ones—
Most recently by me.
Her hair is pale Scandinavian braids;
Her dress—gold-trimmed white,
Her wings—glistening gold embellished cloth,
Her crown—old rhinestones and gold fabric.
She is a semblance of softness and beauty.

She is an unbroken tradition.
Knowing little of what she represents,
I've grown to accept her
And like her better than in years before;
I no longer view her as ugly.
Perhaps I peeked within;
Perhaps we changed together
While she slept in his treasure box
And I slept in his bed.

Constance Howard Moore

A Royal Affair

A celebration of Kingdom citizens,
Each walking in newness of life.
Salt of the earth, vessels of honor,
Children of promise united in Christ.

A royal affair, a wedding feast,
Water turned into fine wine.
A miracle and marvelous thing,
Children of promise united in Christ.

I wrote this poem for a friend's wedding.

A House of Love

Love is precious and much desired;
It costs not a penny,
Is not available for sale,
Yet is worth more than gold.
Love sometimes calls for sacrifice
And always clings to truth.
A house of love is simply built,
Faith is its foundation;
Consideration is its floor;
Its walls are made of hope;
Endurance is its roof.
Decision is the key
That opens doors of gentleness
To rooms adorned with light
And furnishings of restored wood,
Kind words, and peacefulness,
Fresh spring flowers and wool-washed white.
Its windows face throughout the Earth—
And Heaven is its core.

Constance Howard Moore

Section Four:

I Am Alone

I am alone, a dark crystal.
I am alone, purple inside.
I am alone with many.
I am alone, a prism turning,
    Flowering, growing, dying,
        Descending into tiny.
I am alone, floating,
    Abstractly detached,
        Included and excluded.
I am alone with myself,
    With others,
        At home.
I am alone except when
    I'm alone walking
        With my husband.
I am alone, but not when
    I'm alone in a garden
        With flowers.
I am alone in the recesses of my mind.
But I am not alone.
    God is with me.

I took a class on poetry forms. I didn't know anyone in the class and felt out of place, alone, and inferior to everyone there.

Chicken Heart

I feel like a chicken heart,
A puny chicken without a head,
Flopping around,
Helpless and hopeless,
Without reason or sense—
Not knowing where I'm going.

I feel like a weathered old chicken
Dreaming of heights
Falling and tumbling and falling again.
A small dull bird
With an eagle's eyes—
Not knowing where I'm going.

I feel like a floundering chicken
With no head for direction,
No compass to see.
My feet on the earth
Flapping unflown wings—
Not knowing where I'm going.

Self-disappointment, feelings of failure, and fruitless efforts to do better inspired this poem. The chicken idea came from my childhood. When I was a teenager my mother raised chickens. My job was to feed them, gather the eggs, and help clean them after my mother wrung their necks. After their necks were wrung and their heads were gone, they continued to flap their wings and flopped around on the ground wildly for what seemed to me a long time. It's not a picture I can forget.

Out of My Realm

I   A fish out of water—
    How can I swim?
    The dry air is deep—
    Parched wind claims my breath;
    Silently I gasp.

    I'm out of my realm
    Treading deep, dry air,
    A bobbing cork in a desert,
    A fish out of water—
    Drifting in God's reign.

II   I desire to dwell securely
    In a drenching waterfall,
    To breathe water, flow with water,
    And move in a moist water bubble
    With friends and loved ones
    In a sea of kindness.

III I came from a sea,
   From sunshine and salt spray,
   From highlands with balmy air,
   Through burning desolation
   And wilderness places.
   I want to breathe water and be water—
   Gently flowing, buoyant water—
   Quiet water in a refreshing stream.

IV I immerse myself in water-giving life
   To arid regions of my soul,
   Water transforming deserts.
   I want buoyant, swimming, life-giving water
   Enabling in any realm.

I was out of my comfort zone and fighting a lingering cough. The dry heat and my nervousness tended to make my cough worse. I longed for soothing moist air.

Question

I'm from a different place.
Many things I don't understand.
I hear words without meaning.
I scc actions without reason.
I don't understand.
Depression I have known;
But what is depravity?
Neither is of my world.
Life not valued.
Persons not respected.
I don't understand.
Deception I have known.
For what purpose is deception?
Hardship I have known,
But why brutalize another?
For what purpose is cruelty?
These are not of my world.
I see the undesirable loved;
I don't understand.
Some things I can't comprehend.

I only know what I know;
Some of that I don't understand.
I'm on a different channel,
An alien in a foreign land,
A child without genius.
I see people dressed in clothes,
Clothes that I can't see.
Yet I don't see nakedness.
I don't understand.

Unspoken Moments

The conversation races,
Dominated, no gaps,
No spaces, not even a lull.
I'm speechless;
I can't intervene.

Yearning to speak,
Closing my mouth,
Holding my peace,
Words are suppressed,
Kept in my heart.
I've much to say,
Much more to learn.

I'm embarrassed,
Embarrassing,
Considered wrong.
Am I beneath
And unequal?
A lesser one?

Words not worthy,
Dust on a shelf,
Lead in my heart,
Occasional
Internal bleeding.
Screams in the night,
Clouds in my air,
Wedges of separation.

It is good to write.

Inspired by a failed conversation attempt with a very dear loved one, who totally dominated the conversation and didn't leave openings for me to contribute anything.

Human Frailty

We're gods in attitude
In our self-centered deeds.
One standard for ourselves
To satisfy our greed;
One standard for others
To keep them in their place.
We struggle, kick, and push
To win our self-made race.

We're gods in attitude
With blinders on our eyes.
We can't see beyond self
Or past our own desires.
"I" is our attitude;
"I, myself" is our goal;
We view others only
In small, restricted roles.

We're gods in attitude
Singing self-lifting songs.

We seldom claim mistakes
Or admit doing wrong.
We think just of ourselves—
Forget concern and care.
We believe self-made lies—
And proclaim life isn't fair.

Constance Howard Moore

Guilt by Conception

An adult baby cries; an adult baby waits;
An adult baby looks with unopened eyes;
An adult baby places blame.
Mama's guilty, Daddy's guilty,
Others are guilty, too.
An adult toddler's full of lies,
Temper fits and alibis.
An adult toddler walks, rocks in hand,
A ready sling shot circling.
Parents and others are stoned
While maturity waits in a shroud.

Don't mourn what might have been;
Don't dwell on Mom's mistakes.
Why bother condemning Dad?
Proceed beyond what was.

We Sometimes Forget

In a commercialized frenzy,
In the season of Christmas,
We sometimes forget
The gift of all gifts—
The gift of Christ;
The giving of self,
And giving to others as unto God.

In cooking, shopping, and purchasing gifts,
We sometimes forget
What Christmas represents—
Humble beginnings, good news, and joy,
The birth of our Savior,
And Christ living in our hearts.

In celebrating and eating feasts,
We sometimes forget
The most precious gift
And our reason for celebration.

Constance Howard Moore

Short-Term Goals

Life is easier in small pieces,
A day or an hour at a time.
Simple looks good to me,
Doing one thing at a time.

I know it's good to plan ahead,
But short-term goals seem best.
They can be built like blocks
To lean upon and rest.

Short-term goals can be steps,
Easy steps, achievable steps,
Steps toward a greater goal,
Steps that lead to life's best.

A goal achieved feels good.
It can be like having fun,
Like a pat on the back
And a word, well done.

Beware of self-sufficiency
And don't fall into pride,
For we can only do all things
Through our Savior, Jesus Christ.

Let's delight ourselves in our Lord;
Pray and seek and walk with Him.
He knows our heart's desires,
And He is our very best friend.

Smoke

I honor smokers;
I admire their faithfulness and truth.

First thing in the morning,
Last thing at night,
And frequently in between,
Religiously faithful and true,
They offer smoke and sacrifice
To honor their king, the lord of nicotine.

Their example is heard without a word,
They even rise sometimes at night
To offer smoke and sacrifice
In allegiance to their king.

They're seldom deferred by cost involved
Or even time consumed
From giving daily tribute to their king.

Convenience doesn't matter.
They listen and heed as their king calls
And rush to take a smoke
To honor and obey the lord of nicotine.

They congregate in various places
To talk and smoke and honor
The plant that is their king.

Has something gone wrong with the plan?
I thought dominion belonged to man
Over animals, plants, and such as that.
Has dominion gone awry?
But never you mind!

Smokers are a faithful lot!
They give their life and breath
To offer smoke and sacrifice
To the lord of nicotine.

May we, who believe and belong to God,
Observe and be as faithful and true.
If prayer ascended as much as smoke,
What transformations we'd go through.

I wrote this poem in response to a very pro-smoking poem. I realize that smoking is a very real addiction and that many Christians smoke.

A London Rush

Haste, haste, keep up with the pace;
    Move along with your mini-print map,
    A map unreadable for a rat like me.
Enjoy, enjoy, and memorize, so you'll know
    How to go where you want to go
    When left alone and on your own.
Down, down, deep underground
    To a massive maze of ways
    To get where you want to go.
Down, down, deep underground
    To a multiple mess of halls and stairs—
    An amazing maze to a rat like me.
Down, down, deep underground
To tubes and posters and large-print signs;
And some too small to read for a rat like me.
Rush, rush to the escalator.
Stand to the right as the natives run,
    People in a line, one by one,
    Running like running rats
    Running over running water
    Running over running steps

Constance Howard Moore

Without getting their feet wet,
While running past no running signs.
It's a bit much for a rat like me.
Around, around, a hundred more times.
Will they find the lives they left behind?
Are souls lost in gaps and holes?
Is this a type of catacombs?
I thought of the time of the end,
With knowledge increasing
And many running to and fro.
Beware, beware, and mind the gap.
We're going much faster than fast.
Emerge, emerge and see the sights
And masses of people like moving grass,
Or snakes or serpents slithering on.
I'd like the sights with much less people;
It would be better for a rat like me.
Languages, languages, there's ever so many
Like a tower of Babel spilled onto the ground.
Will they ever all speak alike, united as one?
The thought's a bit scary to a rat like me.
I think I'll go home and catch up with myself
And look at daffodils in bloom
And slowly go to a pace more slow,
A pace more agreeable to a rat like me.

I must say I enjoyed all the sights that I saw
And would like to have seen so very much more,
But time just wasn't enough, and I ran out of rush.
I barely slept, and nights seemed long, and now I
need to rest.

*I went on a short walking tour of London with some of
my family. Besides movies and television, it was the first
time I saw people run on an escalator. I would like to go
back and see more at a slower pace. I would especially like
to see some of their gardens in bloom. It was March when
we went. Daniel 12:4 refers to the time of the end.*

We as a Nation

We as a nation
    Seem to have forsaken
        The Lord, our God.
Deception and lies are publicized.
Blind leaders lead the blind.
We proudly proclaim our own way
    And say what's wrong is right
        And what's right is wrong.
We all have sinned and gone astray.
Who will steal?
    Who will kill?
        Who will oppress?
Which babies are doomed?
Where will purity sleep tonight?
Who will tear down?
    And who will build up?
Who will have mercy?
    And who will destroy?
We seemed to have exchanged
    Life-giving living water
        For shallow emptiness.

We seem to wallow in wickedness.
God will judge;
    He knows all;
        He knows our hearts and minds.
We are broken pots of riddled clay,
    Who need hope and repair.
We need the Lord, our God.

Drawing My Picture

I had a picture I wanted to draw,
But I was uncertain of what I saw.
I formed my picture on the clouds in the sky,
And it disappeared in the by and by.
I imagined my picture in the ripples on a lake;
It moved and changed and became a fake.
I painted my picture on my own arm;
There I thought it safe from harm.
Then came the tears of my own life;
My tear-stained picture wasn't right.
I scratched my picture on another's walls;
It seemed safe on an inside hall.
But the roof leaked when a storm came,
And my picture washed away in the rain.
Then I carved my picture in the mud;
Temporarily it seemed like fun.
I made beautiful fluid lines
That vanished in a wink of time.
I drew my picture on the petal of a flower.

My picture wilted along with the flower;
My picture wilted, and so did I;
In desperation I began to cry.
Drawing my picture had become my dream;
I wanted to see it sharp, clear, and clean.
Drawing my picture was my lust.
I even sketched it in the dust
Where the wind quickly blew it away.
Oh, how I longed for my picture to stay.
In a panic I molded it in some clay.
But soon it cracked and crumbled away.
I feared my picture was forever lost.
Then I began to draw upon the Rock;
But my picture couldn't penetrate the Rock.
So I threw myself upon the Rock,
And the Rock imprinted a new picture on me,
A picture of freedom adorned with peace,
A picture new and always fresh,
A picture of love and happiness,
A picture dependent on God, not flesh.

Section Five:

Reflections

A Rose Speaks

A rose smiles
Gently, bold, and unashamed
Unobtrusive and alone
A mild yellow rose
With soft pink edges
Caressing petals
Opening—unfolding
Exposing splendor
A beauty of early fall
A good day greeting
A gracious gift of God
Beckoning
Stop—be still
Appreciate

Happiness Is Freedom

Happiness is freedom
To be real, to bare your soul
And know you are loved;
To face condemnation,
Say you are sorry, and go on.

Happiness is freedom
To speak your mind and forgive,
To be creative and gracious,
To discard burdens
And embrace responsibility.

Happiness is freedom
To choose, to encourage,
To build and rebuild,
To take chances and share,
To be caring and gentle.

Happiness is freedom,
Integrity and peace with God,

Constance Howard Moore

To praise and give thanks,
To cultivate and harvest,
To change and improve.

Happiness is freedom,
Sunshine behind clouds,
A rainbow within,
Wide open pleasant places,
Transcending circumstances.

Consideration

A dagger of words darts from my wound.
Its point felt as it pierces another
And reverberated pain reenters my heart.

A heartfelt hug flew on invisible wings
To embrace without physical arms.
I doubt the recipient knows.

What if hearts were released
To touch the pain and pleasure of one another
And heartfelt hugs transcended space
To embrace
And the sender
And the recipient knew?

What if we overflowed with friendship love
And practiced equality and consideration
In words and in actions?

What if we were honest with ourselves
And no one saw themselves as better
Or beneath another?

What if we were toward others
As we would like them to be toward us?
What if . . . ?

Inspired by hurtful words that I said and immediately
regretted. I wasn't able to take them back.

Peace

Peace for barter is temporal.

True peace is birthed from love;
It sustains,
    Protects,
        Refreshes,
            And forgives.

Peace is a foundation of happiness,
    A way of life,
        A map,
            A road sign,
        Rest within turmoil,
Separation from circumstance,
        Internalized with God,
A state of mind,
    A point of view,
        An attitude.

Constance Howard Moore

Messages of Nature

Roses do not talk
Nor does the giant oak.
Yet they have much to say.
Roses speak of beauty
And the glory of God;
They say hesitate and do not rush;
Rest and enjoy the life you have.
Oak trees speak of majesty,
Small beginnings, and patience.
Wild flowers tell about God's care.
Pine trees say stateliness,
Eternal life, and everlasting love.
Peonies speak of spring loveliness,
Stability, fresh starts, and new life.
Dogwood trees speak of continuity,
Seasons in life, and faithfulness.
Tulips shout surprise, winter's over.
Redbud trees whisper reward.
Cactus utter tolerance,
Uniqueness and different views.
What messages do you read?

Success

I heard my voice crack;
I knew it was a fact.
But read my poem through, I did!

Nervousness filled my throat;
I felt I might even choke.
But read my poem through, I did!

I seemed very short of breath;
My heart beat hard within my chest.
But read my poem through, I did!

Suddenly it seemed hot in the room;
I felt I might possibly swoon.
But read my poem through, I did!

Constance Howard Moore

The Past

Whether the past was good or bad,
    It's not a place to live.
It's a place everyone goes through
    To learn from and forgive.

The past has tentacles to cut;
    It's a place we survive.
The past is a place to release;
    It's not a place we thrive.

The past is a place to grow through;
    It's not a place to stay.
The past is a place for planting
    Some flowers for today.

Raindrops and Tears

Treasure each raindrop
And also each tear;
One cleanses the air,
The other the soul.

Rain waters the earth;
Tears soften the heart.
Clay becomes pliable;
Seeds root and grow.

Constance Howard Moore

Wholeness

Let's blend where we're strong;
Let's blend where we're weak,
Together becoming more complete.
Let's work together and apart,
Using our talents—each one unique.
Let's be individuals and members of a team.
Let's not be an island without a sea.

Seasons and Cycles

All seasons come and go—
Drought, rain, wind, and snow.
Life cycles moving along;
Some weaken; some grow strong.
Decisions are made;
Foundations are laid.
Tomorrows formed today;
Today formed yesterday.
Waves move on every sea.
Winds blow frequently.
All encounter change;
Some are faced with pain.
Living is a process;
Hopefully we progress
As seasons come and go—
Sunshine, storms, and rainbows.

Constance Howard Moore

The Calling of a Crow

The August sun was hot;
The sky was clear, dry blue;
The tree was straight and tall,
Stripped of forest dignity—
Yet dignified and proud,
Holding lines of flowing power.
A crow sat on top of the tree
Calling with all his heart—
Again and again tirelessly—
"Caw, caw, caw."
I saw him calling.
I watched this crow
And noticed as his body moved.
The shoulders of his wings lifted,
His neck and head extended,
And his tail moved with each caw.
I observed his effort.
He called with his whole body,
Perhaps with all his soul.
He spoke wonder to my heart.

I don't know why he called.
Perhaps he called for my attention
Or in allegiance to his Creator,
Saying what God gave him to say,
Repeating one entrusted word.

Purposes

A tree is meant to bear fruit;
A seed should root and grow.
A flower should bloom in time,
As beauty is to show.

The sun should rise and shine each day.
The moon is meant to glow.
Stars are for twinkling,
And cars are meant to go.

A light is for lighting.
A candle is meant to burn.
A mirror should reflect,
And minds are meant to learn.

Clouds should bring rain.
Streams are meant to flow.
Life is meant to live,
And children are supposed to grow.

A poet is meant to write.
A poem is to share.
Words should help communicate,
And to love is to care.

An instrument is meant for use.
A bell is for ringing.
Music is to be heard and enjoyed,
And a song is for singing.

God's Word is meant to light our path.
Prayer is for fellowship.
Jesus was sent for us to receive;
He's God's greatest salvation gift.

Words Are
Like Ripples

Words are like ripples in a sea of air.
Some come to nothing, going nowhere.
Some become great waves of despair.
Some softly wash with soothing care.

Words are like ripples on a sea of air.
Some are storms, cruel and unfair;
They can crush, mangle, and tear.
Some are raindrops of wisdom to help and repair.

Words are like ripples on a sea of air.
Some are hope and some are snares.
Some are rainbows meant to share.
Some rise to Heaven as words in a prayer.

A Collage of Thoughts

Less is often better
 And sometimes provides more.
Less and more are strangely related
 Like balances on a scale.

A seed can lay dormant for a long time
 Then suddenly spring to life.
There's no growth without effort
 On somebody's part.

You cannot see unless you look.
 You cannot find without searching.
You cannot be overcome by good or bad
 Without steps on a path.

There is a way of down then up
 And a way of falling down.
Some right ways seem upside down,
 And others downside up.

Some ways seem completely right,
    But in the end are wrong.
Some weeds can look like flowers,
    And weeds can look like weeds.

Spice

How boring life would be:
With only one kind of tree,
Only one type of flower,
Only one color;
If all pets were dogs
And nothing was wild.

How boring life would be:
With only one point of view,
Only one tone of voice,
Only one culture;
If birds didn't sing
And no one could run.

How boring life would be:
If all books were mysteries,
Without a new thought,
With only one theme;
If life had no challenge
And minds never thought.

Constance Howard Moore

How boring life would be:
Without salt or seasoning,
With no musical tunes
And only one phrase;
If no one had a dream
And children never played.

Controversy

I'm thankful for controversy;
I'm glad it's part of life.
It can be both good and gracious;
It need not stir up strife.
We have the gift of thinking minds—
Why quarrel or become distraught?
I'm glad we don't always agree
On every idea and thought.
Controversy is mind provoking
And inspirational too;
It helps clarify what I believe
And enhances my point of view.
I've purposed in my heart and mind:
I won't be offended by its words,
Though I often think they're weird
And sometimes even absurd!

Beliefs

You've a right to your belief
And I've a right to mine.
May we cause each other to think
And search and seek and find.

May we speak from heart to heart
And try to understand,
And never assault another
With holy book in hand.

May we seek the gift of truth
And become more aware;
May we offer words of wisdom
As wind upon the air.

In the vibrant light of peace
Let's share our points of view,
And give value to each other
In everything we do.

Demon Gods

The offspring of demon gods,
Not limited by race, color, or creed,
Still long to unite with children of light,
Breeding giants of evil and greed,
Spreading shame, anger, fear, and disease.
Often disguised as angels of light
They entice with reasonable, plausible lies,
Causing pain, hatred, destruction, and strife,
Deceptively peddling death and defeat.
They prowl in the darkness of day and night,
Roaring like lions seeking someone to eat.
Beware! No one is exempt from their sight.

Partly inspired by Genesis 6:1–5.

Would You
Have Wisdom?

Wise men still follow Him
    And wise women too
With open minds and open eyes
And willing hearts that say, "I love You,"
    And some with gifts
Of frankincense, myrrh, and gold.
They seek Him and knowledge of truth.
They fear the Lord and know the beginning,
    And know Him who knows the end.
    Wisdom is with Him.
Ask and do not waver;
Believe and see what you receive.
He is the Rewarder of the seeker;
    Those that seek Him, that is,
    Diligently with all their heart.
He knows the future and holds the future;
    He can even change the future.
He is the One with whom there is hope.
He is the giver of all good gifts.

He is the Creator of Heaven and Earth
And He can gently hold your hand
And show you things you do not know.

Inspired by James 1:5–6.

An Enigma

God is in the Heavens
And God is in my heart.
I am in His hands
And He writes upon my heart.

His abilities are endless.
His power is eternal.
His love is everlasting
And His mercies never fail.

His wisdom is infinity.
His knowledge is all encompassing.
His presence is consuming
Like a never-ending fire.

I am drawn into the flames
Of His refining fire
As He holds me in His hands
And writes upon my heart.

I am burned and I am not.
I am safe within His arms.
I am in His Word,
And His Word is in my heart.

His salvation is power to me,
A saving grace for eternity.
He gives to each a measure of faith
And helps us as we humbly pray.

Changing

I see fall colors coming,
Red and yellow in the green.
Greens are beginning to fade
As watercolors splash on trees.

Almost unnoticed, change occurs,
Cooler, shorter days; longer nights.
The grass no longer needs mowing.
Dry brown leaves will soon take flight.

Like whispers, seasons vanish.
Days melt together and run.
A month ago was yesterday.
A year is like the setting sun.

White and gray is in the brown.
The brown is slowly fading.
But life's color is everywhere,
More pleasurable with aging.

Hands

A gardener's hands?
Oh me, oh my, not mine.
But they go with me
When I work in the yard,
When I work with flowers,
When I dig in the dirt.

Ordinary hands?
Yes, that's my hands,
As plain as can be,
Five fingers on each,
Nothing special to see.
They could belong to anyone.

They're my hands,
So they're special to me.
They do lots of hard work.
They do what I expect.
When I garden, they're gardener's hands.
When I rest, they're resting hands.

Constance Howard Moore

A servant's hands?
Could it be?
When I serve, they serve with me.
When I cook, they cook with me.
They work naturally with me;
They don't know what else to do.

Obedient hands?
Like a branch on the vine
Completely in tune.
They go where I go.
They do what I do.
They wouldn't consider less.

We think alike,
My hands and me.
My mind is their mind.
We have unity of thought
And like purposes.
We take pleasure together.

I hold them close;
They are mine for life.
I wash them and care for then.

They are a treasure of help.
They are a gift from God.
We will never part.

A Life of Mistakes?

Was I meant to live a life of mistakes?
To learn and grow through my mistakes
And make the most of my mistakes.
To learn how to fall and how to get up.
To learn to start over again and again.

Was I meant to live a life of mistakes?
To learn I'm no better than anyone else.
To learn, as I needed, to look unto God.
To acquire some compassion and learn to forgive.
To gain understanding and happiness within.

Was I meant to live a life of mistakes?
To learn I can do all things through Christ
And know He's my helper and He gives me strength.
To help me be able to humble myself
And give God the glory and know it's not me.

Was I meant to live a life of mistakes?
To gain a relationship with God, my King,
And sing His praises in everything.

To learn to be able to pass through a trial
And hold His hand as He holds me together.

Was I meant to live a life of mistakes?
I wasn't burned; I didn't drown.
I have some scars, but they're nothing to me.
I suffered some pain and learned a few things.
I've come to know that God is my all in everything.

What Is It That I See?

I think a thought thoroughly through,
    At least I think I do.
I love the light, the little lines,
    Words that say, "I love you."
I like a surprise now and then;
    I'd rather not be sad.
I prefer peace and pleasant things,
    A pause from day to day;
Time to work and a time to think
    And time to meditate,
Time to play and to contemplate.
    What is it that I see?
Sacred things, sunshine, and shadows
    Shrewdly sewn together
Make garments rich in tapestry,
    God's handiwork in man.
God is at work in place and time;
    He sees where we cannot.
I'm humbled that He speaks to me
    And gives me words to write.
God is Supreme; He is Most High;
    He is Almighty God.

What Is Life About?

It's not about prestige
Or the things that we have.
It's not about what God can give;
It's about who God is.

It's not about what we do each day,
Or the medals that we've won.
It's not about our scores on a page,
But the way that we walk with Him.

It's about love and liberty
In relationship with God.
It's about knowing Him and who He is;
It's rejoicing and happiness in Him.

It's not about our names, but His.
It's not about our praise, but His.
It's not about our pride and glory,
But our humbleness in Him.

It's not about our lives
But the life that we have in Him.
It's about being His child and servant
And giving praise and glory to Him.